A Family
CELEBRATION

by Susan Hartley

Table of Contents

How Do We Get Ready for a Special Day?

Here are Rina and Raj.
They live in the United States.

Their grandma was born in India. Their mom was, too. Rina and Raj know many customs from India.

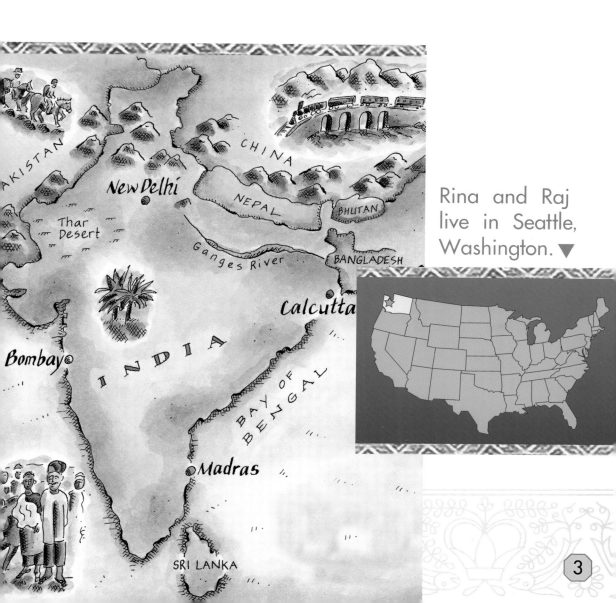

Rina and Raj live in Seattle, Washington. ▼

Today is their grandma's birthday.
The family is getting ready
for a big party.

There will be lots of food at the party. Rina's mom makes jelabi. She loved jelabi when she was a little girl. Now Rina and Raj love it, too.

Jelabi is a sweet dish ▼ people eat as a treat.

Rina and Raj help make other foods that their grandma loves.

They make bread.

They make chicken, too.

They help with the birthday cake.
When the family lived in India,
they did not have cake for birthdays.
Now in the United States, they have cake
as a birthday custom.

Their dad and grandpa put up balloons.

Their aunt brings yellow flowers.
Yellow flowers are special.

Rina has a gift for her grandma.
She can't wait to give it to her.

What Happened at the Party?

It's almost time for the party. Rina and her mother have on saris. Rina's mom used to wear a sari every day when she lived in India.

The balloons are up. The flowers are on the table. The food is ready. Everyone is waiting.

There is a knock at the door.
It is Grandma!

Grandma is very happy to share
her birthday with her family.

Grandma is very happy to share her customs with her family, too.

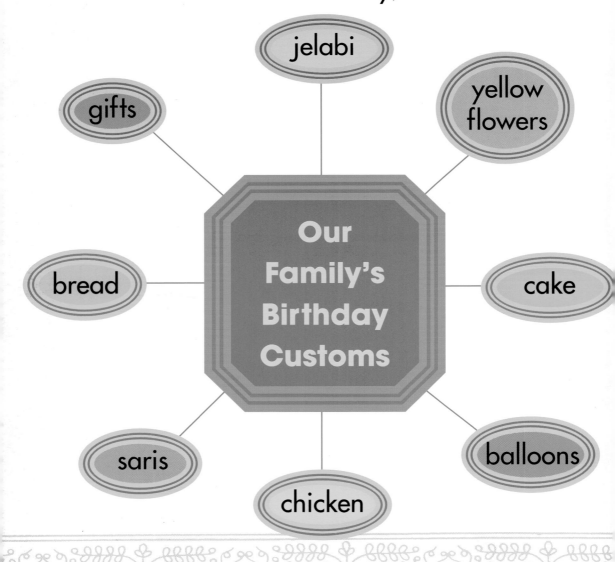

jelabi

yellow flowers

gifts

Our Family's Birthday Customs

bread

cake

saris

chicken

balloons